# THE FUNNIEST NEWCASTLE QUOTES... EVER!

# About the author

Gordon Law is a freelance journalist and editor who has previously covered football for the *South London Press*, the *Premier League*, *Virgin Media* and a number of English national newspapers and magazines. He has also written several books on the beautiful game.

# THE FUNNIEST
# NEWCASTLE
# QUOTES...
# EVER!

## by Gordon Law

Printed in the United States of America
ISBN-13: 978-1544190044
ISBN-10: 1544190042

Photos courtesy of: Featureflash Photo Agency/Shutterstock Inc and Maxisport/Shutterstock Inc.

# Contents

# Introduction

The North East may be the hotbed of soccer, but many of its football personalities have been full of hot air.

Newcastle United players and managers are among those who have kept us amused with countless stupid, yet hilarious remarks that have been talk of the Toon.

None more so than the legendary former England and Magpies boss Sir Bobby Robson who is regarded as one of the game's finest characters.

Whether coming out with bonkers analogies, mixing up his metaphors or simply calling players by the wrong name, his quotes to the media were as memorable as his football achievements.

Kevin Keegan was another Geordie great who made us laugh with barmy statements. His hilarious "I will love it" rant at Sir Alex Ferguson on live TV, as Newcastle battled with Manchester United for the title, is arguably the greatest Premier League sound bite of all time.

There's been popcorn moments on Twitter with born-again 'philosopher' Joey Barton's heated rows, bonehead comments from John Carver, Steven Taylor's jibes at arch-rivals Sunderland and glorious gaffes from Michael Owen.

Many of their classic lines can be found in this unique collection of quotations. I hope you laugh as much reading this book as I did in compiling it.

**Gordon Law**

# THE FUNNIEST NEWCASTLE QUOTES... EVER!

# CAN YOU MANAGE?

"I always thought managers were more involved. But when it comes down to it, I just sit there and watch like everyone else."

**Kevin Keegan on the art of managing**

"I'm like a new stranger to the players."

**Incoming Newcastle boss Joe Kinnear**

"What does my wife think of me still being in management? She doesn't talk to me. Well, she does, but she knows it's pointless."

**Sir Bobby Robson on being a manager at the age of 71**

"The only decisions I'm making at the moment are whether I have tea, coffee, toast or cornflakes in the morning."

**Sam Allardyce after being sacked by Newcastle**

"Today's top players only want to play in London or for Manchester United. That's what happened when I tried to sign Alan Shearer and he went to Blackburn."

**Graeme Souness**

"People say you need coaching badges to be a manager, but when I went to Newcastle my only qualification was a thousand rounds of golf in Spain."

**Kevin Keegan**

"My lad corners me every now and then and tells me what team to pick. He is all of eight. Judging by results, I might be better off listening to him!"

**Manager Alan Shearer**

"I've had a lot of texts from managers saying, 'You must be mad going there'."

**Alan Pardew on joining the club in 2010**

"I have played in five cup finals, I have won the lot. I had over 400 games for Tottenham Hotspur, been manager of the year three times."

**A deluded Joe Kinnear. Won the lot? And it was 196 league games and manager of the year just the once**

"I'm not going to look beyond the semi-final – but I would love to lead Newcastle out at the final."

**Sir Bobby Robson**

"I said straight out, 'If anybody doesn't fancy it, if anybody wants to back-bite, if anybody wants to be negative – there's the door'. [Coach] Steve Stone opened the door, and I told them to leave the room. I told them I was ready for a fight and a challenge, and not one person got up and left."

**John Carver reveals his latest motivational technique**

"There's a good chance I could win French Manager of the Year. It's something I have got my eye on!"

**Alan Pardew manages a large French contingent**

## Can You Manage?

"Well, I don't know if I'm going to live to be 127."

**Sir Bobby Robson when asked if he would stay at Newcastle until they won a trophy**

"You can see why a lot of big names out there didn't have the a*sehole to take this job. You can see why so many people bottled it."

**Joe Kinnear on arriving at Newcastle**

"You hope and you pretend that you know what you're doing."

**Kevin Keegan on becoming Magpies boss**

"I had to remind the players that I've had open heart surgery and there's no way I can have this every week."
**Graeme Souness after Newcastle's thrilling 4-3 win over Manchester City**

"I'm only sleeping about four or four-and-a-half hours a night. I've thought about turning my phone off. You get so many messages; good messages, but it can wear you down."
**John Carver, tired of picking up all those heart-warming texts**

## Can You Manage?

"On my way to the stadium I followed a car with the number plate SOS1. Perhaps someone was trying to tell me something."
**Sir Bobby Robson recalls his first day as Newcastle boss**

"I've only been here five minutes and I'm a cockney. How the hell am I a cockney? I was born and reared in Ireland."
**Joe Kinnear after joining the Tynesiders**

"It's not like it said in the brochure."
**Kevin Keegan on walking out on the Magpies after learning there were no funds to sign Brian Kilcline**

"I still think I'm the best coach in the Premier League."
**John Carver after guiding Newcastle to just nine points from a possible 48**

"No, I don't regret it because I'm the best golfer and the best cricketer in the world as well."
**John Carver after the most laughable "best coach in the league" line**

"Pressure? Sitting at home, watching Coronation Street with slippers on. I'd find that very stressful."
**Graeme Souness**

## Can You Manage?

"I was about to enter a period of life that I can only really describe as a kind of bereavement."
**Sir Bobby Robson is a tad dramatic after being fired as manager in 2004**

"I'm probably the only football manager to be a director of football. I don't know any other ex-managers who have."
**Joe Kinnear, modest as ever**

"I don't want to comment on who or what will take over my job at Newcastle."
**Sam Allardyce after his sacking**

"I heard that silly comment what can I attract. I can open the door to any football manager in the world, anyone. That's the difference. I spend my whole life, picking up the phone, talking to Alex Ferguson, week in, week out, what would you do, what would you do? Pick the phone up at any time of day and speak to Arsene Wenger. I can pick the phone up and speak to any manager in the league, any manager in all divisions. So I don't know what angle they've got. If they want to sit down and argue with me, some of them are talking out their backsides, a load of tosh and I'm not accepting it. It's as simple as that. I've certainly got more intelligence than them, that's for sure."

**Joe Kinnear**

## Can You Manage?

"People think I've been out of the game for 100 years."

**Kevin Keegan in his first press conference since leaving Manchester City manager for Newcastle**

**[At a book signing] Sir Bobby Robson:**

"How many more are there?"

**Robson's PA:** "There's hundreds, Bobby."

**The Newcastle manager signed his next book: 'Bobby Hundreds'**

"Arsene Wenger wrote a nice card and Alex Ferguson said he wanted to see me back in the dugout soon and told me to back one of his horses at Cheltenham. I did and it came fourth. Thanks Alex, just what I needed to relax!"

**Interim manager Joe Kinnear after his heart operation**

"Welcome to The Grey Hair Club."

**Kevin Keegan to John Aldridge on his appointment as Tranmere Rovers manager**

"The only way you're going to win games is by scoring goals."

**John Carver**

## Can You Manage?

"I've told the players to keep playing and watch wrestling or something, but not football."
**John Carver's advice to his team ahead of a big game against West Ham United**

"No one's got an ego. I haven't got an ego."
**Joe Kinnear**

"I intend to be at St James' Park as long as my brain, heart and legs all work... simultaneously."
**Sir Bobby Robson**

"I'm ageing by the day."
**Alan Pardew during a bad run of results**

"He's upset, I'm upset. I hope he comes in for a glass of wine, but I'm told he's gone so it looks like I'm drinking on my own."

**Alan Pardew fails to get a post-match drink with Sunderland manager Martin O'Neill**

# MEDIA CIRCUS

"I haven't resigned; my mother hasn't got chicken pox; I haven't bought a house; I haven't been offered a job with the national team; I haven't been offered a job in America; I'm still here; my wife is OK; my daughter is OK; the groundsman is OK; everybody is OK."
**Ruud Gullit speaking to the press – just days before he stood down as manager**

**Reporter:** "Why do you look so downcast?"
**Sir Bobby Robson:** "I can't sit there laughing, can I? Is that what you want? Ha ha ha – like that? Oh, penalty, ha ha. Oh, it's saved, ha ha. No, it's gone in, ha ha. What do you expect me to look like?"

"That's what it said in the papers – let's hope the papers are right!"

**Kevin Keegan when asked if it was true he had £30m to spend in the transfer window**

**Journalist:** "Do you have a nickname?"

**Shola Ameobi:** "No, not really."

**Journalist:** "So what does Bobby Robson call you?"

**Shola Ameobi:** "Carl Cort."

"I'll snap him in half if I get the chance."

**Graeme Souness about a well-known Evening Chronicle journalist he didn't see eye to eye with**

**Alan Brazil:** "I'm delighted to say we've got Sir Bobby Robson on the end of the phone, fresh from getting his knighthood at Buckingham Palace. Bobby, terrific news."

**Sir Bobby Robson:** "What is?"

**Alan Brazil:** "You know, getting the old sword on the shoulder from Prince Charlie."

**Sir Bobby Robson:** "Eh? [Long pause] Oh yeah... well, it was a day I'll never forget."

"You smell blood, don't you?"

**Ruud Gullit to the media, before he resigned**

"'If' is the biggest word in football, son."

**Sir Bobby Robson to a journalist**

"I have travelled all over the world as a manager. Now this job come up, which I thought was a fairly responsible job, but already they are jumping on the bandwagon. 'Oh watch out Pardo, watch out', but that's the snidey press. That's the people up there or the people round that area that I have upset and they have a grudge so I expect it. It's water off a duck's a*se."

**Director of football Joe Kinnear**

"You'll have to excuse me, I keep burping. I've had a glass of beer."

**Alan Pardew apologises to the press after a win against Stoke**

**The following is an edited transcript of Joe Kinnear's outrageous – and also hilarious – first official press conference as interim manager. He swore 52 times in six minutes.**

**Joe Kinnear:** "Which one is Simon Bird [from the Daily Mirror]?"

**Simon Bird:** "Me."

**JK:** "You're a c*nt."

**SB:** "Thank you."

**JK:** "Which one is Hickman [Niall, from the Daily Express]? You are out of order. Absolutely f*cking out of order. If you do it again, I am telling you you can f*ck off and go to another ground. I will not come and stand for that f*cking crap. No f*cking way, lies. F*ck, you're saying I turned up and [the players] f*cked off."

**SB:** "No Joe, have you read it, it doesn't actually say that. Have you read it?"

**JK:** "I've f*cking read it, I've read it."

**SB:** "It doesn't say that. Have you read it?"

**JK:** "You are trying to f*cking undermine my position already."

**SB:** "Have you read it, it doesn't say that. I knew you knew they were having a day off."

**JK:** "F*ck off. F*ck off. It's your last f*cking chance."

**SB:** "You read the copy? It doesn't say that you didn't know."

**JK:** "What about the headline, you think that's a good headline?"

**SB:** "I didn't write the headline, you read the copy."

**JK:** "You are negative b*stards, the pair of you.

**SB:** "So if I get a new job next week would I take the first day off? No I wouldn't. If I get a new job should I call my boss and tell him I am taking the first day off?"

**JK:** "It is none of your f*cking business. What the f*ck are you going to do? You ain't got the balls to be a f*cking manager. F*cking day off. Do I want your opinion? Do I have to listen to you?"

**SB:** "No, you can listen to who you want."

**JK:** "I had a 24-hour meeting with the entire staff."

**SB:** "Joe, you are only here six weeks, you could have done that on Sunday, or Saturday night."

**JK:** "No, no, no. I didn't want to do it. I had some other things to do."

**SB:** "What? More important things?"

**JK:** "What are you? My personal secretary? F*ck off."

**SB:** "You could have done the meeting Saturday night or Sunday. You could have had them watching videos, you could have organised them."

**JK:** "I was meeting the f*cking chairman, the owner, everyone else. Talking about things."

**SB:** "It is a valid point that was made in there. A valid point."

**JK:** "I can't trust any of you."

**Niall Hickman:** "Joe, no one could believe that on your first day at your new club, the first-team players were not in. No one could believe it in town. Your first day in the office."

**JK:** "My first day was with the coaches. I made

the decision that I wanted to get as much information out of them."

**NH:** "But why Monday, no one could believe it?"

**JK:** "I'm not going to tell you anything. I don't understand where you are coming from. You are delighted that Newcastle are getting beat and are in the state they are? Delighted, are you?"

**NH:** "Certainly not. No one wants to see them get beaten, why would we?"

**JK:** "I have done it before. It is going to my f*cking lawyers. So are about three others. If they can find something in it that is a court case it is going to court. I am not f*cking about. I don't talk to f*cking anybody. It is raking up stories. You are f*cking so f*cking slimy you are raking up players that I got rid of. Players that I had fallen out with. You are not asking Robbie Earle, because he is sensible. You are not asking Warren Barton? No. Because he is f*cking sensible. Anyone who had played for me for 10 years at any level... [but] you will find some c*nt that..."

**Other journalist:** "How long is your contract for Joe?"

**JK:** "None of your business."

**SB:** "Well it is actually, because we cover the club. The club say you are here to the end of October, then you say six to eight games which would take it to the end of November. We are trying to clarify these issues. We are getting no straight answers from anyone. How long are you here for? It is a dead simple question. And you don't know..."

**JK:** "I was told the length of contract. Then I was told that possibly the club could be sold in that time. That is as far as I know. That's it finished. I don't know anything else. But I have been ridiculed. He's trying to f*cking hide, he's trying to do this or that."

**The reporters then discuss how Kinnear had met Newcastle owner Mike Ashley and the executive director Dennis Wise, before continuing...**

**Steve Brenner [from The Sun]:** "We are all grown men and can come in here and sit around and talk about football, but coming in here and calling people c*nts?"

**JK:** "Why? Because I am annoyed. I am not accepting that. If it is libellous, it is going to where I want it to go."

**Newcastle press officer:** "What has been said in here is off the record and doesn't go outside."

**Journalist:** "Well, is that what Joe thinks?"

**JK:** "Write what you like. Makes no difference to me. Don't affect me I assure you. It'll be the last time I see you anyway. Won't affect me. See how we go at Everton and Chrissy [Chris Hughton, assistant manager] can do it, someone else can do it. Don't trust any of yous. I will pick two local papers and speak to them and the rest can f*ck off. I ain't coming up here to have the p*ss taken out of me. I have a million pages of crap that has been written about me. I'm ridiculed for no reason. I'm defenceless. I can't get a point in, I can't say nothing, I can't do nothing, but I ain't going to be negative. Then, half of you, most of you are trying to get into the players. I'm not going to tell you what the players think of you, so then you try and get into them in some way or another, so I've got a split camp or something like that, something like that. It's ongoing. It just doesn't stop."

**Journalist:** "It's only been a week."

**JK:** "Exactly. It feels more like a year."

**Journalist:** "It's early days for you to be like this."

**JK:** "No, I'm clearing the air. And this is the last time I'm going to speak to you. You want to know why, I'm telling you. This is the last time. You can do what you like."

**Journalist:** "But this isn't going to do you or us any good."

**JK:** "I'll speak to the supporters. I'm going to tell them what the story is. I'm going to tell them. I don't think they'll interpret it any different, I don't think they'll mix it up, I don't think they'll miss out things. I mean, one of them last week said to me... I was talking about in that press conference where you were there, I said something like, 'Well, that's a load of b*llocks...'"

**Journalist:** "'B*llocks to that' is what you said."

**JK:** "B*llocks to that. And what goes after that?"

**Journalist:** "That was it."

**JK:** "No it wasn't, no it wasn't. What was after it? I don't know if it was your paper, but what went after it?"

**Journalist:** "I don't know."

**JK:** "It even had the cheek to say 'b*llocks to Newcastle'."

**Journalist:** "I didn't write that."

**JK:** "That was my first f*cking day. What does that tell you? What does that tell you?"

**Journalist:** "Where was that? Which paper said that?"

**JK:** "I've got it. I can't remember. It was one of the Sundays, not a Saturday. It was a Sunday."

**Journalist:** "But you didn't say that to the Sundays, you said that to us. That was during the Monday press conference."

**JK:** "I'll bring it in and show it to you. Why would I want to say that?"

**Journalist:** "Are you saying that someone has reported you saying, 'b*llocks to Newcastle'?"

**JK:** "Yes. Lovely."

**Journalist:** "I don't know who's reported that."

**JK:** "I'll tell you what, I'll bring it in."

**Journalist:** "That's obviously going to damage you. That's not a good thing. But I don't think someone's done that. We have to have some sort of relationship with you."

**JK:** "So have I. But I haven't come in here for you lot to take the piss out of me. And if I'm not flavour of the month for you, it don't f*cking bother me. I've got a job to do. And I'm going to do it to the best of my ability. I'm not going to spend any more time listening to any crap or reading any crap. Stick to the truth and the facts. And don't twist anything."

**Journalist:** "You know, you know the game..."

**JK:** "Of course I know, but I don't have to like it."

**Journalist:** "Today we'll print the absolute truth, that you think we're c*nts, we can all f*ck off and we're slimy. Is that fair enough?"

**JK:** "Do it. Fine. F*cking print it. Am I going to worry about it? Put in also that it'll be the last time I see you. Put that in as well. Good. Do it."

"He just said, 'Will you go and do the press for me?' That was it. I was actually eating a pie at the time."

**Assistant John Carver on Alan Pardew ducking out of his post-match media duties**

"You guys probably write the truth. Then in the office the editors chop out the important things. Like facts."

**Kevin Keegan**

# BOARDROOM BANTER

"Sir John [Hall] was a multi-millionaire when I joined Newcastle. Now he's just an ordinary millionaire."
**Kevin Keegan after splashing out £15m for Alan Shearer**

"If, like me, you like a gamble now and again, then what price a flutter on us reaching that top six?"
**Mike Ashley, in December 2008. Newcastle were relegated at the end of the season**

"Robson the man I don't really know. I just know Robson the manager."
**Freddy Shepherd on Sir Bobby Robson**

"The fans are mugs. Newcastle girls are dogs. Me, I like blondes, big bust, good legs. I don't like coloured girls. I want a lesbian show with handcuffs."

**Freddy Shepherd, recorded in secret by the News of the World**

"Our fans like people like Keith Gillespie – they relate to people who like to have a drink and get into trouble."

**Douglas Hall**

"You simply do not sack Bobby Robson."

**Freddy Shepherd, days before sacking his manager**

"I never said I was an expert in football clubs. I was just a fan, although a very wealthy fan. But I'm not so wealthy now."

**Mike Ashley after Newcastle's 2009 relegation**

"You should only say good things when somebody leaves. Robert has gone. Good."

**Freddy Shepherd on Laurent Robert joining Portsmouth**

"I quite liked Mike Ashley. I thought, 'Yeah, this could be good'. But no, it was a nightmare, an absolute living nightmare."

**Kevin Keegan on his return in 2008**

"The Newcastle chairman Sir John Hall went on the record to claim that Les Ferdinand would be leaving Newcastle 'over my dead body'. I wonder if he is still alive."
**Les Ferdinand**

"Derek Llambezee was the director of football."
**Joe Kinnear. It's "Llambias" and he was actually the managing director, while Kinnear was the director of football**

"Him and his fat mate should be sh*tting it if I decide to write a book. There'll be no holding back on those two muppets."
**Joey Barton blasts Derek Llambias**

"[Mike] Ashley offered me his helicopter. It seemed really generous until I got an eye-boggling invoice. It was business after all."
**Joey Barton after Mike Ashley allowed him to ease his commute from Southampton, following his release from prison in 2008**

"Alan Shearer is boring – we call him Mary Poppins. He never gets into trouble."
**Freddy Shepherd**

"Do I care what Alan Shearer says? When he was manager we were relegated after picking up five points from eight games."
**Derek Llambias hits back at Alan Shearer**

"Sam [Allardyce] would be a fool to let it happen and the guy who goes in would be a fool to accept it. The chairman, who is not a fool, would be a fool to go and do it, too."

**Kevin Keegan on rumours he is set to become Newcastle's director of football**

"Let's kill off the rumours that Ossie Ardiles' job is on the line. If he ever leaves it will be of his own volition."

**Sir John Hall sacked the manager days later**

"We haven't fallen out. You can't fall out with somebody you never talk to."

**Kevin Keegan on Sir John Hall**

"[Mike Ashley] loves football but he sometimes can't understand how it works and it confuses and upsets him, and when he is upset he does things that aren't brilliant for the football club."
**Alan Pardew**

"I saw Mike's shirt. He asked me to sign it but I refused!"
**Kevin Keegan after seeing Mike Ashley wearing a shirt with 'King Kev' on the back**

# BEST OF ENEMIES

"I've kept really quiet, but I'll tell you something, he went down in my estimation when he said that. But I'll tell ya – you can tell him now if you're watching it – we're still fighting for the title, and he's got to go to Middlesbrough and get something, and... and I tell you honestly, I will love it if we we beat them... love it!"

**Kevin Keegan's famous TV rant at Sir Alex Ferguson, as the race for the 1995/96 title with Manchester United started to heat up**

"When I'm warming up, their fans' veins are popping out of their necks. It's like I've done something to their family or something."

**Steven Taylor on Sunderland supporters**

"Graeme Souness went behind my back right in front of my face."

**Craig Bellamy. But which was it?**

"I have been sold like a slave for a bag of gold."

**Hughie Gallacher on joining Chelsea in 1930**

"I'd rather go and collect stamps than stick on that shirt."

**Steven Taylor when asked if he would play for Sunderland**

"Most footballers are knobs."

**Joey Barton**

"Someone's going to get a slap today, just make sure it's not you!"

**Joey Barton to James Troisi after he didn't take his apology for a late tackle in training with the good grace that was intended**

"We have said it all the time, we wouldn't take any of their players."

**Steven Taylor takes a swipe at Sunderland**

"[Mike] Ashley, one thing, you don't understand Newcastle, you don't understand the fans and the city. We deserved more. We are the Geordie nation."

**Jonas Gutierrez rants at the club owner**

"I hated it. The f*cking fans were a bag of sh*t, the players weren't worth a light. I used to be at the dogs all the time. I bought a couple of greyhounds and thought, 'F*ck football'."

**Forward Billy Whitehurst**

"My reputation will always precede me to the day I die. For some people, that probably can't be quickly enough."

**Joey Barton says it how it is**

"He's a flatterer. And his final ball is pathetic. Pathetic. He fools the public but he doesn't fool me."

**Sir Bobby Robson on Steve McManaman**

"If they knew more about football than we do, there would be 50,000 players and 22 spectators."

**Bill McCracken on getting abuse from the fans**

"When I arrived, the fans called me a thieving Spaniard and a bloody gypsy who was robbing the club's cash."

**Marcelino**

"It was handbags at half-mast, really."

**Alan Pardew on a bust-up between the Newcastle and Southampton coaching staff**

"I loved Newcastle – until Gordon Lee took over."

**Malcolm MacDonald on why he left for Arsenal in 1976**

"Tell Alex [Ferguson] we're coming to get him."

**Kevin Keegan after leading Newcastle to promotion in 1993**

"Shut yours, you f*cking old c*nt."

**Alan Pardew to Manchester City manager Manuel Pellegrini during a touchline row**

"He can play in our reserves!"

**Steven Taylor on Sunderland's Adam Johnson**

"As long as my family don't boo me when I walk through the door, I couldn't care less!"

**Michael Owen after getting abuse from the fans**

"He's like the guy who sits in the front row and listens to the teacher. I certainly don't lose any sleep when I play against him."

**Joey Barton makes fun out of Gareth Barry**

# MANAGING PLAYERS

"Congratulations, I've heard a lot about you. But whatever you do, don't get injured."

**Incoming Newcastle manager Sir Bobby Robson to injury-prone Kieron Dyer before the England v Luxembourg game in 1999**

"When Andy Carroll first appeared on the scene he was a tall skinny kid and his coordination was all over the place. He reminded me of a giraffe."

**Glenn Roeder**

"He's not the Carl Cort that we know he is."

**Sir Bobby Robson**

"All right, [Craig] Bellamy came on at Liverpool and did well, but everybody thinks that he's the saviour, he's Jesus Christ. He's not Jesus Christ."

**Sir Bobby Robson**

"Sometimes you want [Gabriel] Obertan to open his legs and do something a bit exciting."

**Alan Pardew**

"Gary Speed has never played better, never looked fitter, never been older."

**Sir Bobby Robson**

"Andy O'Brien has an horrendous nose, the poor lad. It is massive, it is black and blue and it is awful."

**Sir Bobby Robson**

"I told him Newcastle was nearer to London than Middlesbrough, and he believed me."

**Kevin Keegan on signing Rob Lee**

"In the first half he took a corner, a poor corner, which hit the first defender, and it took him 17 minutes to get back to the halfway line."

**Sir Bobby Robson on Laurent Robert**

"He's got this terrific little engine, I don't know where he gets his petrol from – I could do with some of that."

**Sir Bobby Robson on Kieron Dyer**

"It's a long time since I've seen a player who you feel would kick his granny to win, and that's lovely – though not for the granny."

**Glenn Roeder on Steven Taylor**

"Laurent Robert said I was picking the wrong team – at the time I was, because he was in it."

**Sir Bobby Robson**

"We can't replace Gary Speed. Where do you get an experienced player like him with a left foot and a head?"

**Sir Bobby Robson**

"That's it with [Michael] Owen – you shoot holes in him and he comes back for more."

**Kevin Keegan**

"Titus [Bramble] makes one mistake every game. If he could just correct that bad habit, he'd be one of the best defenders in England."

**Sir Bobby Robson**

"I think they've got some magnificent midfield players: Tiote. Ben Afri [Hatem Ben Arfa], Yohan Kebab [Yohan Cabaye], Sissoko are very solid... Shola Amamobi [Sammy Ameobi] is getting better and better, he's a young kid. And Galteirez [Jona Gutierrez]."

**Joe Kinnear**

"I don't want your houses, your helicopter or your money. I just want to borrow that for an hour to visit my wife."

**Kevin Keegan to Les Ferdinand after seeing 'Big Les' walk out the shower for the first time after training**

"Shay [Given] pulled out with a knee injury as did Insomnia... Insomnia... er, Charlie."

**Joe Kinnear mispronounces Charles N'Zogbia's name**

"OK, I got a little tongue-tied, but if I had a pound for every time I've mispronounced a player's name down the years, then I'd be a very wealthy man indeed."

**Joe Kinnear after calling Charles N'Zogbia "Insomnia"**

"He's the only man I know who could start an argument with himself."

**Sir Bobby Robson on Craig Bellamy**

"On the coach, Kieron Dyer suddenly shouted, 'Stop the bus! I've left my earring in the dressing room'. Can you imagine a player telling Bill Shankly, 'Stop the bus, Bill, I've lost an earring."

**Sir Bobby Robson**

"David Ginola has just handed in a transfer request. The handwriting was beautiful."

**Kenny Dalglish**

"You couldn't do that to Marcelino, could you son?"

**Sir Bobby Robson to a magician who had made his wrist watch disappear at a charity function**

"It would have been nice if both players had maybe shaken hands with each other."

**Sir Bobby Robson on Kieron Dyer and Lee Bowyer fighting**

"I don't know what will happen with Shola [Ameobi] in the future, he could become Prime Minister one day with his personality."

**Alan Pardew**

"Now we've got [Gareth] Southgate..."

**Sir Bobby Robson having just signed Jonathan Woodgate**

"We've got great speed in the team, not just Gary Speed, but great speed!"

**Sir Bobby Robson**

"[Shane] Ferguson has a left foot you could peel oranges with."

**Alan Pardew on the Newcastle academy player**

"Titus looks like Tyson when he strips off in the dressing room, except he doesn't bite and has a great tackle."

**Sir Bobby Robson on Titus Bramble**

"Jermaine Jenas is a fit lad – he gets from box to box in all of 90 minutes."

**Sir Bobby Robson**

"He's a player that can reach heights that other players can't reach – that Heineken player if you like."

**Alan Pardew on Hatem Ben Arfa**

# LIFESTYLE CHOICE

"Warren Barton's the best-dressed player I've ever seen. He even arrived for training in shirt, trousers, shoes and his hair's lovely. We call him The Dog, as in the dog's b*llocks."
**Robert Lee**

"I haven't a clue how many women I had [on holiday in Ayia Napa] – four or five maybe. But I regret it deeply."
**Kieron Dyer**

**Journalist:** What made you decide to come to Newcastle?
**John Hendrie:** "McEwan's Best Scotch."

"We don't want them to be monks. We want them to be football players, because monks don't play football at that level."
**Sir Bobby Robson after it was reported that Newcastle players had been seen partying in nightclubs**

"When he first came he wanted to get a fishing boat so they took him to Tynemouth the first weekend he was here. He took one look at the North Sea and said, 'F*ck that!'"
**Nick Emerson, Tino Asprilla's interpreter**

"I would have given my right arm to be a pianist."
**Sir Bobby Robson**

"If we invite any player up to the Quayside to see the girls and then up to our magnificent stadium, we will be able to persuade any player to sign."

**Sir Bobby Robson**

"I'll be bringing the pigeons up to Newcastle with me, but I'll have to bring them up in the car. They're not good enough to find their own way here yet!"

**Duncan Ferguson**

"Vaya ciudad – what a town!"

**Columbian star Tino Asprilla after visiting Newcastle's Bigg Market**

"I use Clinique on my face, especially in Newcastle because the wind is so bad."
**Warren Barton**

"Tino need new car!"
**Faustino Asprilla to the manager of the club's sponsored cars after he wrote off his Range Rover**

"I don't think she knows I'm in Germany because we play Bayer Leverkusen that night. She might have arranged a dinner party. I will have to tell her. She doesn't know, honestly."
**Sir Bobby Robson on his wife arranging his 70th birthday celebrations**

"People say I'm cocky because I have two cars and a diamond watch. But that means 90 per cent of footballers are cocky."

**Kieron Dyer**

"I was never too aware of his problems with booze, but he was still a hell of a player when he had them."

**Alan Shearer on Tony Adams**

"Mr Willie, I am f*cking starving. Can I have fish and chips?"

**Mirandinha to manager Willie McFaul after the Brazilian made his debut at Norwich**

"I did not know of Hull. I know nothing. Maybe with my satellite navigation I could find it. I would have no idea where it is on the map, though."

**Obafemi Martins**

"Sitting eating sushi in the city, incredibly chilled out reading Nietzsche."

**The 'intellectual' Joey Barton tweets**

"We are meant to be these hard-headed, money-obsessed professionals but we are still little boys at heart. Just ask our wives."

**Rob Lee, oh yeah?**

"I was asked which one I'd choose, Viana or Viagra? That's easy. Saturday afternoon, Viana. Saturday night, Viagra."

**Sir Bobby Robson on playing Hugo Viana**

"I have discovered Newcastle Brown Ale and my ambition is to speak Geordie as well as Peter Beardsley."

**David Ginola**

"I'd like to put a sticker on my head that says 'Doing fine thanks, don't ask'."

**Michael Owen on being approached by Newcastle fans in town**

"I can say that he did get married and that it is his second marriage. This is nothing unusual. He is a Muslim."

**Cheick Tiote's agent Jean Musampa confirms the midfielder has two wives – more than he has goals (one) for Newcastle**

"Not a problem Les, but I'm not too sure she'll be happy stopping with me knowing what I've got and knowing what you've got to offer."

**Lee Clark to Les Ferdinand when 'Big Les' asked his teammate to hide Dani Behr in his flat while he got rid of the paparazzi**

"We have got all sorts of different books for [Andy] to pick from. He might like Peppa Pig – or there is a monkey one."

**Kevin Nolan wants Andy Carroll to read to his kids**

# CALL THE MANAGER

"It started badly even before kick-off. I have to go on record to say it was an altercation... You know what I'm like, I'm not a shrinking violet, am I? We had words with each other..."

**The charming John Carver on his clash with Newcastle fans away at Southampton**

"I would be in danger of being whipped off to the old nuthouse if I started saying it."

**Kevin Keegan, in his second spell as boss, rules out Newcastle's title chances**

"It's Fantasy Island stuff."

**Glenn Roeder is delighted to be leading his side in the Intertoto Cup**

"During the week, there were three or four managers mentioned. Gerard Houllier, there were so many, I lost count. Sven-Goran Eriksson was in there as well."

**Joe Kinnear is not the best at adding up**

"I took him off because he wasn't hungry enough for his hat-trick."

**Arthur Cox on why he substituted two-goal star Chris Waddle**

"I've only got two words for how we played out there tonight – not good enough."

**Sir Bobby Robson**

"I spoke to Mike Williamson at half-time and had a few choice words. I thought he'd done that on purpose – it looks like he did. The ball was off the pitch – he had no need to make the challenge. He will miss two games now. Is it an easy way out?"

**John Carver's astonishing claim that Mike Williamson deliberately got himself sent off at Leicester**

"I like the number four. I think we should sign him."

**Ruud Gullit to coach John Carver after watching Lee Clark play for Sunderland – a year after Newcastle had sold him to their fierce rivals**

"White socks look brighter and good teams wear them. I tried it during the season and we played some good stuff. You feel better and the players wanted it."

**Ruud Gullit managed to change his team's socks from black to white... and they then lost at home to Everton**

"We've enjoyed the ride, we've paid the money, got the ride, got off the tramcar – let's go again. We can do better."

**Sir Bobby Robson after Newcastle exited the Champions League with a defeat to Barcelona**

"We probably frightened them into life and they killed us for it."

**Steve McClaren after Newcastle took the lead against Manchester City but ended up losing 6-1**

"I'd like to smash the ball into a referee at 200mph and see if he can get out of the way."

**Sir Bobby Robson on Nolberto Solano's red card for hand ball at Tottenham**

"I'm not urging anything. I'm just urging players to put in better performances."

**Alan Pardew**

"I can't fault the lads for their effort again in a hot, warm climate. They were hot conditions, and we kept going and going and going. Next week is a huge game for this football club. I'll tell the players to keep away from the TV and going online, to keep them focused on preparation."

**John Carver blames defeat against QPR on the 'scorching' 18C heat and the internet**

"He doesn't swear, Shola, and said, 'Are you going to send me off?' being sarcastic. And he did."

**Alan Pardew on Shola Ameobi's red card against Liverpool**

"Tottenham can offer him the chance to play in a cup final, they are in Europe – and the only way we're going to get into Europe is if we get on a ferry."

**Kevin Keegan on attempting to sign defender Jonathan Woodgate**

"Sad and miserable, but very effective."

**Sir Bobby Robson on Wimbledon after they won 2-0**

"He had some curried goat and maybe that was why he was fuelled up today."

**Alan Pardew after Papiss Cisse's two goals against Liverpool**

"We mustn't be despondent. We don't have to play them every week – although we do play them next week as it happens."

**Sir Bobby Robson after losing to Arsenal in the league – days before meeting them again in the FA Cup**

"The most important thing is the players get a good pre-season under their belts. The most important thing is that the club has to come straight back up."

**That's two most important things then Chris Hughton?**

"If you ask the Peterborough supporters today how magical the FA Cup was midway through the second half, they will tell you it's the best thing since someone invented mercury."

**Sir Bobby Robson**

"I don't know whether people are going to buy me a drink or throw them at me – that's the sort of week it's been."

**Alan Pardew after a 4-4 draw against Arsenal**

"We used to have Shaka Hislop on our books but I've never heard of Shakira."

**Sir Bobby Robson after finding out the pop star was staying in the same Barcelona hotel**

"It was more like common assault than anything you expect to see on a football field."
**Sam Allardyce is furious with Juventus keeper Gianluigi Buffon's challenge on Andy Carroll during their friendly fixture**

"If I'm honest, I have to admit there's a chance they're just not listening to me."
**John Carver reckons the players are ignoring him after an eighth straight loss**

"We're developing our youth policy."
**Kenny Dalglish on old boys Ian Rush and John Barnes joining Newcastle**

"I was brought here to clean up and that's a bad job. We won four games in a row, but I knew the sh*t would come."

**Ruud Gullit**

"We've got a Mickey Mouse ref doing nothing."

**Joe Kinnear on referee Martin Atkinson after defeat away to Fulham**

"It is a lot harder when you are 4-1 down than when you are 4-1 up."

**Kevin Keegan after losing to Manchester United**

"Manchester United dropped points, Liverpool dropped points, Chelsea dropped points, Everton dropped points, so in a way we have not lost anything at all really, although we dropped all three."

**Sir Bobby Robson**

"We don't seem to be able to get through this tie [third round stage]. For the last three years I don't know, it's science against me."

**Alan Pardew after Cardiff dump Newcastle out of the FA Cup third round**

"I don't care if they ban me or fine me. Fine me what you like – I will pay it and I will still be right. I know I am right. Never in all my career have I seen a referee influence a game like that. He destroyed it and I blame him for us losing the game. I can't blame it on myself, my team or Aston Villa. It was the referee and nothing else."

**Ruud Gullit fumes at referee Uriah Rennie for sending off Alan Shearer**

"If I have to move on from Newcastle, hopefully it will be to somewhere else."

**Joe Kinnear**

"It was a great result and it might stop people saying Newcastle have not won under Kevin Keegan."

**Kevin Keegan on winning against Fulham for his first victory in his second spell back at Newcastle**

"Will he be okay for the Wigan game? I'll have to check his tweets and see."

**Alan Pardew after Jose Enrique revealed on Twitter he would miss the Tottenham match due to injury – before Pardew announced his squad for it**

"They expect me to put the ball in the net, stop the headers going in, stop the opposition from scoring. I can't affect that. I can't get on the end of the corner and head the ball clear which would have kept us one up at half-time. I can't do that."

**John Carver on getting flak from the supporters**

"C'mon Toon Army! The club and I need your total involvement!"

**The bizarre final line in Rafa Benitez's statement to the fans on his appointment – which was very unlikely to have come from his lips**

"I didn't put Remie Streete on there to make a point. He really was my only defender and he shouldn't be anywhere near my bench – that's the truth of it."
**Alan Pardew rates his player highly then**

"For the first time we have two central defenders who have been pillars and not pillocks."
**Bobby Robson on Darren Peacock and Steve Howey**

"We'll play you anywhere – Hackney Marshes – we're not frightened."
**Kenny Dalglish to the mighty Stevenage Borough after their pitch was deemed unfit**

"I actually thought we contained him quite well."

**Alan Pardew on Gareth Bale who scored twice in a 2-1 win for Tottenham**

"Until we're out of the Champions League we're still in it."

**Sir Bobby Robson**

"I could sign a bad player every day between now and 31st January. There are plenty out there."

**Glenn Roeder is fed up at not landing his transfer targets**

"On a scale of one to 10, it's a minus 10. I can't accept it. I wish the players had as much determination and fight as I had. We can talk about systems and players but if we're not willing to compete, get your head on to the ball and risk getting an injury, you won't get anywhere."

**John Carver is furious after a 3-0 defeat away at Leicester**

"We don't have to play them every week, although it seems like we have this week."

**Kevin Keegan after Newcastle's second loss in a week against Arsenal**

"We've made an improvement, and I think from fourth to third at the top of the Premiership is a massive step. It's not so massive when you're 20th and you finish 19th or if you're 19th and you finish 18th or even if you finish 18th and then finish 17th. But I think when you move up a place at the top, it's quite massive, so we've had an improvement."

**Sir Bobby Robson**

"We are protecting our asset. There's a big value in Kieron Dyer... so I am protecting the asset... it was my decision to protect that asset and not risk him today because he is a valuable asset for Newcastle United."

**Sam Allardyce on his asset**

"Well, we got nine and you can't score more than that."
**Sir Bobby Robson after Newcastle beat Sheffield Wednesday 8-0 in his home debut as manager**

"Yes I did receive a two-match ban for calling a ref Coco the Clown but I'm down to one after today."
**Joe Kinnear starts his Newcastle reign with a touchline ban, which was held over from four years earlier**

"It was all good up until when it kicked off."
**Alan Pardew after losing at Southampton**

"Two things struck me straight away. The standard of Jose's English and the fact that he was a nice-looking boy. Too good-looking for my liking."

**Sir Bobby Robson on his first impressions of Jose Mourinho**

# A FUNNY OLD GAME

"Nobby Solano discharged himself from hospital after the Tottenham game and he's driving, living the life and aware of who he is."

**Sir Bobby Robson**

"And they were lucky to get none."

**Len Shackleton after a 13-0 win over Newport County**

"I picked up an injury and spent quite a lot of time on the bench. One of the supporters knitted me a cushion to sit on, which said, 'Reserved for Brian Kilcline'."

**Brian Kilcline**

"Even the referee shook my hand. He could have given me a penalty – that would have been even better!"

**Alan Shearer after breaking legend Jackie Milburn's scoring record**

"All you've got to do is score a goal. These foreigners are all the same, they'll collapse like a pack of cards – they've no gumption."

**Manager Joe Harvey's team talk in the 1969 Fairs Cup second leg against Ujpest Dozsa**

"My son Mathieu called it a 'Ninja goal'. This is a result of me playing on his PlayStation – it inspires me to try the craziest of things."

**Laurent Robert on his wonder strike against Fulham**

"I will bust a gut to play in any game."

**Michael Owen after recovering from a stomach op**

"The match for them is a bit like people down south going to the theatre. They want to be entertained."

**Kevin Keegan on the Newcastle fans**

"I'll switch off the TV and wait for someone to ring me with the result."

**Kieron Dyer won't be watching if he's injured for England's World Cup squad**

"We dealt with everything they threw at us, apart from the three goals we conceded."

**Steven Taylor after losing to Chelsea**

"As soon as I walked into the ground I was greeted by the statue of former striker Malcolm MacDonald."

**David Ginola gets the wrong legend... he meant Jackie Milburn**

"The manager said at half-time if I got six, he might give me a Mars bar. I'll have to go out and buy my own now, won't I?"

**Alan Shearer on Sir Bobby Robson after he scored five times in the 8-0 win over Sheffield Wednesday**

"Alan is struggling to walk and he can't use crutches because his hand is in plaster. We may have to put him in a wheelchair."

**Sir Bobby Robson on Alan Shearer**

**Physio:** "How are you?"

**Mirandinha:** "I'm very well, thank you. How are you?"

"It is a basket-case of a club... I will resist the urge to write a book, although I think it will sell more copies than JK Rowling!"

**Steve Harper**

"Newcastle have always had a poor pitch in winter. We don't have the better weather. My lawn up here isn't as good as my lawn in Ipswich."

**Sir Bobby Robson**

"A new club is like having a new girlfriend – you don't have feelings straight away."

**Michael Owen**

"You can't force people to sit down even if they have a seat. They want to sing and, unless you're Val Doonican, you can't do that sitting down."

**Kevin Keegan on the Newcastle home crowd**

"If the Arsenal players don't like being tackled, they should go and play basketball or netball or one of the other games."

**Joey Barton after a 4-4 draw with the Gunners**

"Mirandinha will have more shots this afternoon than both sides put together."

**Malcolm MacDonald**

"Alan Shearer has done very well for us, considering his age. We have introduced some movement into his game because he has got two good legs now. Last season he played with one leg."

**Sir Bobby Robson**

**Michael Owen:** "I worked my nuts off to get back from injury.

**Reporter:** "How are you feeling now?"

**Michael Owen:** "My groin's a bit sore."

"He's been feeling his groin for a week now."

**Boss Alan Shearer on why Obafemi Martins didn't play against Middlesbrough**

"I'm really pleased I don't have to miss three games. Having said that, two of them were at Leeds and Arsenal, so I was thinking about not appealing when I found out it was those games."

**Alan Shearer on having his red card rescinded**

"It is frustrating. However, and people will probably laugh, I know I'm not injury-prone."

**Michael Owen**

"I wouldn't be bothered if we lost every game as long as we won the league."

**Mark Viduka**

"Last season [Fabio] Capello didn't come to see Newcastle when we had the best defensive record up to Christmas. The gaffer went to some event and Capello was there, and he said, 'You should come up and see Taylor'. And Capello said, 'I'm all right for midfielders'."

**Defender Steven Taylor**

"Arsenal are streets ahead of everyone in this league, and Manchester United are up there with them, obviously."

**Craig Bellamy**

"The first time, I heard my name but I didn't understand the words. So I looked on the internet. They chant after a goal, sometimes just after a run!"

**Yoan Gouffran on the supporters**

"My father was a footballer – he only ate peas because they were round."

**Fabricio Coloccini**

"They say it's because I'm a sexy boy. The English are crazy!"

**Yohan Cabaye on his 'Dreamboat' nickname given to him by Newcastle's fans**

"I may have looked calm but my backside was going some."

**Alan Shearer on his successful penalty against Tottenham in the 1999 FA Cup semi-final**

"I never thought it would take so long for me to have a chance to put it on. It does smell. I have only cleaned it once or twice."

**Jonas Gutierrez on the Spider-Man mask he finally got to pull out of his pants when he scored his first goal for the club**

"I did go down easily – I've been hit harder by people at school... I have made a meal of it."

**Joey Barton after Gervinho was shown a straight red card for slapping him**

# SAY THAT AGAIN?

"We need to realise we're now the head of the mouse and not the tail of the lion. It's a Spanish expression. So, when you are in the Premier League, you are the tail of the lion and some people are happy being the tail of the lion, some prefer to be the head of the mouse."

**Rafael Benitez**

"The big thing about Newcastle is there is only Newcastle in Newcastle."

**Joey Barton**

"The players have got to pick themselves up and we've got to help pick them up."

**Kevin Keegan**

## Say That Again?

"I don't believe in superstitions. I just do certain things because I'm scared in case something will happen if I don't do them."

**Michael Owen**

"There are knives going in my back and arrows flying around my head but I don't think some people have any idea what we have to do to keep the ship solvent."

**Bobby Robson**

"We had Ameobi to Ameobi – which is almost like a song – for the second goal, which was nice."

**Alan Pardew**

"If we could bring some silverware to the club that would be a nice little rainbow at the end of a dark tunnel."

**Terry McDermott**

"I'm looking for a goalkeeper with three legs."

**Sir Bobby Robson after keeper Shay Given is nutmegged twice by Ipswich striker Marcus Bent**

"The circus came to town but the lions and tigers didn't turn up."

**Kevin Keegan after losing at Manchester United**

## Say That Again?

"I don't know whether, one, he wants a number two, or two, whether I would like to be one."

**Alan Shearer when asked if he wanted to be Kevin Keegan's assistant**

"I tried to push him away with my head."

**Alan Pardew on head-butting Hull's David Meyler**

"David Batty is quite prolific, isn't he? He scores one goal a season, regular as clockwork."

**Kenny Dalglish**

"We need a point as soon as possible, the tooter the sweeter."

**Sir Bobby Robson**

"I bumped into a lady today when I was popping out for my lunch and she said, 'You are looking after my nine-year-old at the moment'. I said, 'Well, there is a route to the first team'."

**Alan Pardew**

"Yeading was a potential banana blip for Newcastle."

**Sir Bobby Robson**

## Say That Again?

"We're in a dogfight and the fight in the dog will get us out of trouble. We are solid behind each other, and through being solid we will get out of trouble and, if that fails, then we will be in trouble, but that's not the situation here. We'll all get in the same rowing boat, and we'll all pick up an oar and we'll row the boat."

**Sir Bobby Robson**

"You never sell the fur of a bear before you shoot it. I have brought my cannon with me."

**Ruud Gullit on trying to sign Ibrahim Ba**

"Nobody hands you cups on a plate."

**Terry McDermott**

"We've got to batten down the hatches, plug a few leaks and get the ship sailing again."

**Sir Bobby Robson**

"I know the players I want. It is like I have them in the fridge waiting to come out."

**Ruud Gullit**

"Titus Bramble had a very good game – which will silence all the boo-boys – and put them in the drink. And we can get on with our lives."

**Sir Bobby Robson**

## Say That Again?

"We go home with some new experience, and certainly for some of our players, because they won't get that time on the ball they had tonight in a Premier League game. Sometimes you can be uncomfortable with time, trust me."

**Alan Pardew**

"Somewhere in those echelons of NUFC, they have decided, I am persona non grata."

**Joey Barton tweets after Newcastle announced he was free to leave**

"I believe Geordies in key posts at this club give you a potentially vital extra one per cent that non-Geordies don't."

**Freddy Shepherd**

# TALKING BALLS

"Take them for f*cking everything, son. Take them for every penny!"

**Paul Gascoigne to Lee Clark before he went to sign his first professional contract**

"One accusation you can't throw at me is that I've always done my best."

**Alan Shearer**

"At Newcastle I was older than the manager, older than the assistant manager, older than the physio and the club doctor – which must be some sort of record."

**Stuart Pearce**

"Next morning I decided to have it out with the manager [Ruud Gullit]. Dunc [Duncan Ferguson] had beaten me to it and the door to the manager's office was already off its hinges when I got to the training ground."

**Alan Shearer**

"Hairy mot!"

**Mirandinha greeting people after being told by Paul Gascoigne that "hairy mot" was "hello"**

"He calls me Shay Brennan."

**Shay Given on Sir Bobby Robson**

"If anyone ever hears that Kevin Keegan is coming back to English football, they can laugh as much as I will. It will never happen."

**Kevin Keegan on moving to Spain in 1985**

"Monday, Tuesday, W*nkday, Thursday, Friday, Saturday and Sunday."

**Paul Gascoigne teaching new Brazilian striker Mirandinha the days of the week**

"I don't know what I'd have become if I hadn't been a footballer; I wrote down 'dustbin man' on a careers questionnaire at school till my dad made me change it to 'joiner'."

**Alan Shearer**

"I love Kenny [Dalglish]... Very easy to talk to, very hard to understand."

**Gary Speed**

"I've known him since he was 6ft 3ins!"

**Steve Harper on Andy Carroll**

"Sam Allardyce knows what the club needs. He's done it at both ends."

**Damien Duff**

"He makes players 10 feet taller."

**Rob Lee on Kevin Keegan's magical powers**

"Don't you dare put it on quick spin or I'll f*cking brae the lot of you."
**Gazza to the United apprentices in 1988 before he climbed into an industrial dry cleaner at Benwell Training Ground**

"I've never wanted to leave. I'm here for the rest of my life, and hopefully after that as well."
**Alan Shearer believes in the afterlife?**

"Ronnie, f*ck off."
**Mirandinha to the man who made the drinks and sandwiches after training at Benwell, after being told by Gazza that "f*ck off" was "coffee"**

"That's the way I am and I always will be. After all, I kick Laurent Robert in training – and he's one of our players."
**Andy Griffin**

"F*ck you! F*ck you!"
**Words heard most weeks from Faustino Asprilla on discovering his socks and shirts had been cut up after training at Maiden Castle in Durham**

"He convinced us we were playing downhill towards our fans in the second half."
**Tim Krul on Alan Pardew's motivational technique**

**Tommy Cassidy:** "Is Aiden McCaffery Irish?"

**Gordon Lee:** "No, he's a Geordie, born and bred."

**Tommy Cassidy:** "You sure?"

**Gordon Lee:** "Yes, definitely."

**Tommy Cassidy:** "How can anybody with a name like Aiden McCaffery not be Irish? Well your surname is Lee, boss, but you're not Chinese!"

"He gets so upset when he misses a chance in training. Sometimes you will see him arguing with himself for five minutes about how he missed it."

**Tim Krul on Papiss Cisse**

"I would like to compare them to a Duracell battery, though I think even a Duracell battery would conk out before those two."
**Steven Taylor on Jonas Gutierrez and Gabriel Obertan**

"I'll be shaving the moustache off now that we have won. There are a few of the lads desperate to get it off. It is either the end of my moustache or the end of my relationship, so I'm glad it is going."
**Joey Barton explains why he celebrated his goal against Aston Villa by waggling fingers over his moustache**

"I know you've signed for United, but do you think it's the wrong United? Do you not think Rotherham is where you're supposed to be and you've taken a wrong turn somewhere?"

**David Batty is unimpressed with new signing Des Hamilton**

"Happy birthday – any chance of a rise?"

**Alan Shearer's message in Sir Bobby Robson's 70th birthday card**

Printed in Great Britain
by Amazon